THE ART OF SOUL-WINNING

LECTOR HOUSE PUBLIC DOMAIN WORKS

THE ART OF SOUL-WINNING

JOHN WILMOT MAHOOD

ISBN: 978-93-90215-06-5

Published: 1901

LECTOR HOUSE LLP
E-MAIL: lectorpublishing@gmail.com

THE ART OF SOUL-WINNING.

(SPECIALLY ADAPTED FOR PERSONAL WORKERS.)

BY

J. W. MAHOOD, EVANGELIST,

Author of "The Missing Wheel Found," and joint-author of
"The Young People's History of Methodism."

"And he brought him to Jesus."

PREFACE.

Never was there such great need for a mighty, Pentecostal revival in all our Churches; and the key to such a revival is earnest personal work. But the membership of the Churches are not prepared to enter upon this work. Multitudes know nothing of a personal Pentecost. Many are utterly indifferent. They do not realize their opportunity and responsibility before God. If they did, the revival would come at once.

With the hope that many professing Christians may be awakened to duty, and hear God's call to personal work in soul-winning, this little volume is written.

Let the pastor see that a copy is put into every home one month previous to the time set for special revival-meetings. Let him secure a pledge from the people to read the study for each day, commit the memory verses, and meditate upon the Scripture suggested.

Once each week, either at a special meeting appointed for this purpose, at the week-night prayer-meeting, or at the young people's devotional meeting Sunday evening, let the studies for the week be reviewed and the memory verses recited. Short talks may also be given on each topic by persons previously selected.

When the entire Church membership shall begin to think and speak upon these vital themes; when the spirit of grace and supplication shall take the place of formality and worldly desire; when the Holy Ghost of Pentecost shall come upon the waiting, praying Church, then the times of refreshing will be sure to come from the presence of the Lord, and the perishing multitudes will be saved.

Sioux City, Iowa.

CONTENTS

THIRD WEEK -THE SOUL-WINNER'S EQUIPMENT.
"COMPLETELY FURNISHED."

FOURTH WEEK -THE SOUL-WINNER'S METHODS.
"THAT I MAY, BY ALL MEANS, SAVE SOME."

FIRST WEEK-THE SOUL-WINNER'S MOTIVE.

"FOR THE LOVE OF CHRIST."

STUDY I.

FOREWORD AND APPEAL.

Memory Verse: "And they that are wise shall shine as the brightness
of the firmament; and they that turn many to righteousness as the
stars for ever and ever." —(Dan. xii, 3.)

Scripture for Meditation: Matt. vi, 19-23; Rev. iii, 14-22.

Fred B— — was a medical student. He was stricken, with that dreaded scourge,
consumption. The physicians advised a trip to the mountains. During the first few
months among the Rockies he improved rapidly, and hope and ambition flamed
anew; but it was only a brief respite from suffering before the final collapse. Lying
in a Denver hospital, he was visited by some consecrated young people, who sang
and prayed with him. He yielded himself to Christ, and the peace of God filled his
heart.

They brought him home to a little Iowa city to die. The day after his arrival the
pastor was summoned to his bedside, when the young man related the circum-
stances of his conversion. The pastor said, "Then you are not afraid to die?" "No,"
said he, *"not afraid, but not ready."*

When asked why he was not ready, he replied: "I have done nothing for my
Master. I have won no souls for him. Could I have six months more to live that I
might bring some souls to Jesus, and thus not go into his presence empty-handed,
I would be satisfied to die. *I am not afraid to die, but not ready."* Just then the door of
the room opened, and the dying boy's father, an old, white-haired man who had
been absent from home and had not seen his son since his return, came in. The old
man was not a Christian. Then occurred a pathetic scene. The young man threw
his arms about his father's neck, and drew him down upon his knees at the bedside, urged him to give himself to God, and then, with shortening breath, uttered
such a prayer of intercession as is seldom heard. The old man sobbed aloud, yielded to Christ, declared his faith, and the dying boy had won one soul for his Master.
In a few hours he had gone into the presence of the King; *but not empty-handed.*

O ye to whom God has given the strength and vigor of manhood and woman-
hood, and who have pledged your allegiance to the Christ of Calvary, are you winning any souls for your Master? Or are you going into his presence *empty-handed*?
What if in the judgment-day it shall be seen that some souls who might have been
saved have been lost through your neglect? What if it shall then be seen that the
crown of many stars which you might have won is given to another? And what, if

in the great day of his appearing you shall be found, having gathered no sheaves and *empty-handed*?

STUDY II.

THE LORD'S COMMAND.

Memory Verse: "Go ye into all the world and preach the gospel to every creature." —(Mark xvi, 15.)

Scripture for Meditation: Ezek. xxxiii, 1-11.

By the Master's final words to his disciples the obligation is laid upon every Christian to be a soul-winner. "Ye shall be my witnesses," is the risen Lord's message to all his followers. No one is excused. "Follow me," said Christ, "and I will make you fishers of men." And when his face was set toward Calvary, he said to the Father, "As thou hast sent me into the world, even so have I also sent them into the world." By the mouth of the prophet Ezekiel, God distinctly says that, if we neglect "to warn the wicked from his way, that wicked man shall die in his iniquity; but his blood will I require at thine hand." We are all *sent*, and if we shrink or excuse ourselves from our great mission we shall come into condemnation.

The unsaved multitudes know that every Christian should be an ambassador for Christ, and when we fail to do our duty we are condemned in their eyes as well as before God. A writer in the *Epworth Era* says:

"A college professor who was noted among his fellow-teachers for his habit of addressing young men upon their personal relations to Christ, was asked by one of his fellow-professors, 'Do they not resent your appeals as an impertinence?' He replied: 'No! Nothing is of such interest to any man as his own soul and its condition. He will never resent words of warning or comfort if they are prompted by genuine feeling. When I was a young man, I felt as you do. My wife's cousin, a young fellow not yet of age, lived in our house for six months. My dread of meddling was such that I never asked him to be present at family worship, or spoke to him on the subject of religion. He fell into the company of a wild set, and was rapidly going to the bad. When I reasoned with him I spoke of Christ. "Do you call yourself a Christian?" he asked, assuming an astonished look. "I hope so," I replied. "But you are not. If you were, he must be your Best Friend. Yet I have lived in your house for six months, and you have never once named his name to me; no, he is nothing to you!" I have never forgotten the rebuke.'"

STUDY III.

BY PERSONAL EFFORT.

Memory Verse: "And he brought him to Jesus." —(John i, 42.)

Scripture for Meditation: John i, 35-45.

Have you ever noticed that much of the work which the Master and his disciples did was "personal work?" Some of our Lord's greatest sermons were preached to one person. The apostles were all won individually. Turn to your Bible now, and read the account of the visit of Nicodemus to Christ, and of the meeting with the woman of Samaria at the well. If you take the time to follow this theme through the Gospels and through the Acts of the Apostles, you will be sure to see that the work of winning souls for Christ by personal effort is the work of every Christian.

And a conviction of this is the greatest need of the Church to-day. It is the key to the twentieth-century revival. The world would be evangelized in this generation did each professing Christian win only one soul each year for Christ; and the great social and labor problems of the day would be speedily solved were the great Christian Church actively engaged in leading men and women to Jesus of Nazareth. Mightier than the influence of great sermons and fine music and splendid ritual is the influence of a life consecrated to personal effort in seeking the lost.

That remarkable soul-winner, Dr. J.O. Peck, now translated, said: "So great is my conviction of the value of personal effort, as the result of a lifework of winning souls, that I can not emphasize the method too strongly. If it were revealed to me from heaven by the archangel Gabriel that God had given me the certainty of ten years of life, and that as a condition of my eternal salvation I must win a thousand souls to Christ in that time; and if it were further conditioned to this, that I might preach every day for the ten years, but might not personally appeal to the unconverted outside the pulpit; or that I might not enter the pulpit during these ten years, but might exclusively appeal to individuals, I would not hesitate one moment to make the choice of personal effort as the sole means to be used in securing the conversion of one thousand souls necessary to my own salvation."

Dr. Theodore Cuyler once said concerning the three thousand souls he had received into Church fellowship during his ministry, "I have handled every stone."

STUDY IV.

TROPHIES 2OF PERSONAL EFFORT.

Memory Verse: "And he that is wise winneth souls." —(Prov. xi, 30, R.V.)

Scripture for Meditation: 2 Cor. v, 14-21.

Is it not a suggestive fact that nearly all those men who have shone brightly in the galaxy of martyrs, preachers, and reformers in the Christian Church through the centuries have been won to Christ by the personal effort of some consecrated life? Think of some in our own age.

Dwight L. Moody, when a clerk in a store, was visited by his Sunday-school teacher, who put his hand upon the young man's shoulder and talked to him about Christ; and Mr. Moody says, "I had not felt I had a soul till then."

Colonel H.H. Hadley, who has kneeled and prayed with over thirty-five thousand drunkards, declares that one of the agencies which led him to Christ was a brief interview with Chaplain (now Bishop) McCabe on a railway-train in Ohio just after the Civil War.

Lord Shaftesbury, one of the greatest Christian philanthropists of the nineteenth century, was won for Christ in early boyhood by the effort of Maria Willis, a servant-girl in his father's home.

The conversion of Diaz, the great Cuban evangelist, was due to the faithfulness of a consecrated young lady of Brooklyn. She found him in a hospital at the point of death, procured a Spanish New Testament, read to him the words of mercy and invitation, pointed him to Christ; and he went back to his own country, a flaming herald of the gospel.

J. Wilbur Chapman, one of the most successful pastor-evangelists of this generation, says that while in a revival-meeting, when a boy, his Sunday-school teacher touched him on the elbow, and said, "Do you not think you had better stand?" and that one touch, as much as anything else, pushed him into the kingdom.

Joseph F. Berry, whose name is a household word in the Methodist Episcopal Church, was led to Christ by two young friends who took the young printer to his father's barn, and held a prayer-meeting with him, which resulted in a glorious conversion.

STUDY V.

THE WORTH OF A SOUL.

Memory Verse: "For what is a man profited, if he gain the whole world, and lose his own soul? Or what shall a man give in exchange for his soul?" — (Matt. xvi, 26.)

Scripture for Meditation: Luke xv, 1-10.

What is a life worth? What is your life worth? What is the life of your son or daughter or mother or wife worth? What would you take for a life? But if the life of a dear one be worth so much to you, what must be its value in God's sight, who sees to what depths a soul may plunge and to what heights it may rise? It may be a small matter to you that in yonder saloon is a man dissipated and drunken. But what if he were your father or brother or husband? It may be a very small matter to you that the boy whom you met on the street is puffing a cigarette and wears already upon his face the marks of an evil life. But what if he were your boy or your brother? Yet, in God's sight, his life is as valuable as if he were your boy or your brother; and every soul is of infinite worth.

Jesus Christ set a high estimate upon human life when he left his Father's throne and came into this sin-cursed world to suffer and die that he might redeem us from death.

The Church of to-day needs a new vision of the worth of a soul. We need to stand beside Calvary and see the price that was paid there for human life.

John Keble, the poet-preacher of the English Church, said that the salvation of one soul is worth more than the framing of the Magna Charta of a thousand worlds.

It was meditation upon the words of the memory verse of this study that fired the souls of Ignatius Loyola and Francis Xavier with a holy enthusiasm to rescue the perishing multitudes. Had their successors and disciples been, filled with the same enthusiasm, and kept themselves free from the machinations of politics, they would have long since evangelized the world, and Jesuitism would not have been "the scandal of Christianity."

STUDY VI.

THE DEATH OF A SOUL.

Memory Verse: "Let him know, that he which converteth the sinner from the error of his way shall save a soul from death." — (James v, 20.)

Scripture for Meditation: Luke xvi, 19-31.

What is death—the death of a soul? What is it to die eternally? In the passage for meditation our Lord gives us a glimpse into the realms of death. Surely the Son of God is not trifling here; nor does he speak to confuse. For a moment the curtain is drawn, and we see what is actually transpiring in the future world. In these days there is a disposition in some quarters to make light of the future punishment of the wicked. Some preachers are dumb upon the awful punishment of sin, or preach only half a gospel, saying, as Bishop Warren puts it, "You must repent, as it were; be converted, in a measure; or you will go to hell, so to speak."

But Christ did not speak with any uncertain sound about the future punishment of the impenitent. He is authority. Take your Bible and read such passages as Matt. xxv, 41, 46; Matt. viii, 12; Luke xvi, 23; John v, 29.

In the light of these words, we must see that the death of a soul means eternal separation from God, from mercy, and from heaven.

And yet how indifferent we are concerning the unsaved multitudes all about us who are drifting into a hopeless eternity. The Church needs a vision like that of the little lad in Olive Schreiner's "Story of a South African Farm," who, waking at midnight, sees multitudes drifting over the precipice into eternal night, and throws himself on his face on the floor, crying out in the agony of his burdened heart to God to have mercy.

Some one tells of a shepherd in the Far West who, on a dark, stormy night, found three sheep missing. Going to the kennel where the faithful shepherd-dog lay with her little family, he bade her go to find the sheep. An hour afterwards she returned with two. When these had been put in the fold, he said, "One sheep is yet missing. Go!" The faithful dog took one mute look of despair at her little family, then was off in the dark and the storm. In two hours she had returned with the lost sheep, but was torn and bleeding, and, as she staggered toward the kennel, fell dead at the door. But if a poor, dumb brute, with no immortal hope, be obedient, even unto death, what shall we say of men and women who know the destiny of the soul, and whom the King of kings has bidden seek the lost, yet are disobedient, indifferent, and thoughtless as to the dying multitudes about them?

STUDY VII.

THE SUPREME MOTIVE.

Memory Verse: "For the love of Christ constraineth us." —(2 Cor. v, 14.)

Scripture for Meditation: 1 Cor. xiii, R.V.

But the supreme motive in all our efforts to win others should be "the glory of God." Possessed of an undying love for him who first loved us, we will have an inspiration to seek the lost for whom he gave his life. And all our efforts shall be, as Paul puts it in his letter to the Ephesians, "unto the praise of his glory."

> "The love of Christ doth me constrain
> To seek the wandering souls of men."

Love never faileth. Love knows no impossibility. He who works for wages and he who works for love live in two different realms. A lot of men were entombed in a coal-mine, and great crowds gathered to help clear away the earth and rescue the miners. An old, gray-headed man came running up, and, seizing a shovel, began working with the strength of ten men. Some one asked to relieve the old man. "Get out of the way," he cried; "I have two boys down there."

Love will triumph; and he whose heart throbs with love to Christ will find real joy in rescuing from sin those who are the purchase of his blood, *that his name may be glorified.*

Study his life of self-sacrifice. See again his suffering for sinful men. Linger in Gethsemane, and behold the agony of Calvary. Then your heart will begin to throb with love to him "who first loved us."

Get a new vision of your crucified, but now risen, Savior, until the beauty of his matchless life charms your heart and you are ready to say:

> "Come, and possess me whole,
> Nor hence again remove;
> But sup with me, and let the feast
> Be everlasting love."

Then you will possess the highest motive that moves human hearts, and personal work in soul-winning will become a real delight.

SECOND WEEK -THE SOUL-WINNER'S LIFE.

"YIELD YOURSELVES UNTO GOD."

STUDY VIII.

A DEFINITE EXPERIENCE.

Memory Verse: "Verily, verily, I say unto thee, except a man be born again, he can not see the kingdom of God." —(John iii, 3.)

Scripture for Meditation: John iii, 1-15.

In a prayer-meeting a young lady was asked, "What is the first thing we must do if we would win others to Christ?" She replied, *"We must live holy ourselves."* She was right. Just as the telegraph wire must be insulated, so must the life of him who expects to be the messenger of God be insulated from the old life of sin before he can hope to carry the loving messages of the gospel to other souls.

This implies a definite experience of conversion. He who would engage in this most fascinating of all work must have nothing short of an inner consciousness of sins forgiven and of the presence of Christ in his life. He must be able to say, like Andrew and like Philip of old, "I have found him." He must know what it is to have "a new heart" and to have peace with God.

William Butler, the veteran missionary and soul-winner, now translated, wrote the author of these studies a letter, in which he said:

"First and foremost, I thank God for a true conversion. When I got religion, I got it good and thorough. Christ became everything to me. The law of sin, or temptation to worldly conformity of any kind, was completely eradicated from my heart; and from that hour to this the law of Christ has fully satisfied my soul, and made me gloriously free and independent of the world and its maxims and pleasures. And now, after fifty-five years' enjoyment of peace with God and humble devotion to his service, I bless him that I ever gave him my heart and devoted myself to his work. I am happy. The consoling comforts of the grace of God are with me by day and by night, and the blessed future is radiant with the hope of being 'numbered with the saints in glory everlasting.'"

In these days of compromise and doubt we need to have as definite an experience of salvation as had William Butler. He who would win others to a new life must himself possess that life, and know it, being able to say with Paul, "I know whom I have believed."

STUDY IX.

A COMPLETE SURRENDER.

Memory Verse: "I beseech you therefore, brethren, by the mercies of God, that ye present your bodies a living sacrifice, holy, acceptable unto God, which is your reasonable service." —(Rom. xii, 1.)

Scripture for Meditation: Rom. vi, 1-13.

John Wesley said, "Give me one hundred preachers who fear nothing but sin and desire nothing but God, and I care not a straw whether they be clergymen or laymen, they alone will shake the gates of hell and set up the kingdom of heaven upon the earth."

A life surrendered to God will be an invincible life, while the life only partly surrendered will know nothing but defeat. Someone says that, in the transfer of property, any reservation implies, also, reserved rights. If a man sells a ten-acre lot, and keeps a yard square in the center for himself, he has a right of way across what he has sold to get to his reservation. And if, in our surrender, we keep back anything, "that constitutes the devil's territory, and he will trample over all we call consecrated to get to his own." Therefore a complete surrender of the life to God is absolutely necessary.

To the rich young man who came to him, Jesus said, "One thing thou lackest." He demanded an unconditional surrender of every interest of his life. But the young man was not willing to make the surrender, and went away sorrowful. Of every man and woman Jesus asks the same surrender. But many now wander off in the darkness of formality and doubt because they are not willing. Three things are implied in such a surrender: (1) An acknowledgment of the Divine ownership and human stewardship in all temporal affairs; (2) A complete submission of the will to God; (3) The supremacy of Jesus Christ in the heart and life, so that the interests of his kingdom are first, always, and everywhere.

There is an old story of a monk who, having been disobedient to the rules of the monastery, was told he must die. They took him out into the graveyard, stood him upright in a grave, filled in the earth about his feet. Then they asked, "Are you dead yet?" He said, "No." The earth was then filled in about him to his waist, and the question again asked. He replied, "No." Then they filled in the earth until he was covered, all but his head, and could scarcely breathe. When asked if he would die, he replied, "Yes, I will give up; I will die." So may we die to the old life of self and sin, and live the new life of entire surrender to our risen Lord!

"If Christ would live and reign in me,
I must die, I must die.
Like him I crucified must be,
I must die, I must die.
So dead that no desire may rise,
To pass for good, or great, or wise,
To any but my Savior's eyes, —
Let me die, let me die."

STUDY X.

THE SPIRIT'S WITNESS.

MEMORY VERSE: "The Spirit Himself beareth witness with our spirit that we are children of God." —(Rom. viii, 16, R.V.)

SCRIPTURE FOR MEDITATION: 1 John v, 1-15.

When the life has been wholly surrendered to God, and Christ, the crucified and risen Savior, is enthroned in the heart and confessed before men, then the blessed assurance of our sonship with God will be clear and joyous. No longer shall we say, "I hope I am a Christian," or, "I am trying to be a Christian;" but, like Paul, we shall exclaim, "I know whom I have believed."

The witness of the Spirit will give a holy confidence to the soul-winner.

> "What we have seen and felt,
> With confidence we tell."

Much of the timidity and reluctance shown by Christians toward personal work may be traced to a refusal or neglect to live the surrendered life and have the clear assurance of acceptance with God.

This direct testimony to our adoption is given only by the Holy Spirit, and given only to believers because they are the sons of God. It is God's seal which he places upon his own, and we then no longer receive the spirit of bondage unto fear; but we receive the spirit of adoption whereby we cry, Abba, Father. The voice of God is heard in the soul bearing witness to our acceptance, and then the fruit of the Spirit speedily follows in the life to corroborate the inner voice and "give unmistakable confirmation to the testimony which was primary and direct."

To some, this assurance comes like a sudden flash from the sky; to others, like the gentle breathing of the evening zephyr. But it comes, *it surely comes*; and no soul should be satisfied until it comes; for it is essential to a useful, joyous life. Look up now, and with eager expectancy await the "blessed assurance."

> "Why should the children of a King
> Go mourning all their days?
> Great Comforter, descend and bring
> The tokens of thy grace.
>
> Assure my conscience of her part
> In the Redeemer's blood;
> And bear thy witness with my heart,

That I am born of God.

Thou art the earnest of His love,
The pledge of joys to come;
May thy blest wings, celestial Dove,
Safely convey me home!"

STUDY XI.

EVERY WEIGHT.

Memory Verse: "Wherefore seeing we also are compassed about with so great a cloud of witnesses, let us lay aside every weight and the sin which doth so easily beset us, and let us run with patience the race that is set before us, looking unto Jesus, the author and finisher of our faith." —(Heb. xii, 1, 2.)

Scripture for Meditation: 1 Cor. viii, 9-13; ix, 24-27.

We hear much about "personal liberty" in these days, and, to hear some talk, one would think that personal liberty was a gift to be selfishly guarded rather than to be sacrificed for the good of others. But Paul, the apostle, sacrificed his liberty for the sake of others; so did Onesimus, the Christian slave. Surely those professing Christians who make "personal liberty" their plea for engaging in some form of worldly amusement (such as dancing, card-playing, or theater-going), and those who are given to some filthy habit (such as the use of tobacco), have not studied the life of Jesus, or of Paul, or of Onesimus.

If there were no other reasons why these things should be renounced, that they injure our influence as soul-winners would be sufficient; for who ever heard of a man or woman who engaged in these forms of questionable amusement becoming illustrious as a soul-winner? To say the least, they are "weights," and must be laid aside.

In a revival service, a lady rose, and, with tears raining down her face, said: "I have taught a Sunday-school class of sixteen young men for three years, and have not seen one of them converted. I believe I know why, and now confess my sin. Being a teacher in the city schools, I thought I must see a Shakespearean play, and went to the theater one night. I saw several of my class there, and they all seemed to be looking at me as if surprised. Next day I met some of them, and they confessed surprise that I was at the theater. I have been conscious from that time that I had lost my influence to win these young men to Christ." Within one week after this confession was made this lady had won seven of her class for the Savior.

A young lady, once a society belle and fond of worldly amusements, consecrated her life to the Lord's work. In a rescue mission she was asked to speak to a poor wreck of a man who had been a gambler. He looked at her suspiciously as he asked, "Do you play cards, or dance, or go to the theater?" "No, not now," she replied. "Well, then you may talk to me; but I won't listen to one word from you fine folks who are doing on a small scale the very things that brought us poor wretches to where we are." And the young lady afterwards said she had found more real joy in leading that lost soul to Christ than she had ever found in the pleasures of the world.

Lay aside every weight; lay aside every weight, just now.

STUDY XII.

PRAYER.

Memory Verse: "The effectual fervent prayer of a righteous man availeth much." — (James v, 16.)

Scripture for Meditation: Gen. xxxii, 24-30; Luke xi, 1-13.

Nothing is more essential to the soul-winner than prayer. Prayer will generate a spiritual atmosphere in the individual life. The prayers of many will generate a spiritual atmosphere in a community. In answer to prayer, the Holy Spirit will do his office, and produce such pungent conviction of sin that men will carry out, as on the day of Pentecost, "Men and brethren, what shall we do?"

In the Life of Mr. Finney it is related that, during a revival at Rome, New York, the air seemed surcharged with Divine power. A sheriff, who had laughed about the meetings, came over from Utica. He felt this strange influence when he crossed the old canal, a mile west of town. When he sat in the hotel dining-room, he had to get up and go to the window two or three times to divert his attention and keep from weeping. After dinner he hurried away, but was afterwards converted.

See what spiritual triumphs and great revivals the early Church witnessed; but the secret of it all was that "they continued steadfastly in prayers." Why is it that to-day many have so little courage and so little power to win others to Christ? They neglect prayer. "They that wait upon the Lord shall renew their strength; they shall mount up with wings as eagles; they shall run, and not be weary; they shall walk, and not faint." How little time we spend daily in prayer! Study the life of Paul, and Savonarola, and Catherine of Siena, and Martin Luther, and John Knox, and see how they all gave themselves continually to prayer, and so prevailed. All they who have become illustrious as great soul-winners have been, without exception, men and women mighty in prayer. They came to understand that God's storehouses of wisdom, prayer, and grace are inexhaustible, and with the key of prayer they unlocked every door.

Prayer avails for the salvation of others when every other means seems to fail. The disciples spent ten days in prayer. Then came Pentecost and a revival that brought thousands into the kingdom. John Livingstone, with a few friends, spent a whole night in prayer, and the next day five hundred persons gave themselves to Christ. Two sisters agreed to spend the night in prayer in behalf of an unconverted brother. That night, although twenty miles away, the young man tossed on his bed in agony of conviction, and next day started for home, and found salvation.

Prayer is omnipotent; and, if we would see the kingdom of Christ come speedily in the world, we must have a great revival of prevailing prayer.

STUDY XIII.

FAITH.

Memory Verse: "Verily, verily, I say unto you, He that believeth on me, the works that I do shall he do also; and greater works than these shall he do; because I go unto my Father." — (John xiv, 12.)

Scripture for Meditation: Heb. xi.

Not the mystery of faith, nor the philosophy of faith, does the soul-winner need to study; but the simplicity, the childlikeness of faith. To believe God implicitly is to have victorious faith. "I can do all things through Christ which strengtheneth me," said Paul; and everywhere in the Bible we find the clear teaching that "God and one make a majority." To realize this in one's own life is to live the victorious life.

But perhaps we should distinguish between trust and saving faith. Trust gives the life to God; faith takes from God that which he has promised in his Word. Trust is continuous; faith is a definite act. "Faith is the giving substance to things hoped for, the evidence of things not seen." (Heb. xi, 1.)

It is true that we walk by faith now; but faith has a clear eye. Faith can see the clouds full of chariots and horses. Faith can see legions of angels marshaling themselves for our defense. Faith can see that every promise of God is steadfast, and will surely be fulfilled, and can claim its fulfillment.

> "Faith, mighty faith, the promise sees,
> And looks to that alone;
> Laughs at impossibilities,
> And cries, 'It shall be done.'"

Of Barnabas it is said, "He was a good man, and full of the Holy Ghost and of faith." The fullness of faith will make unbelief and moral darkness impossible in the soul, and will generate a triumphant confidence in God.

To have faith is to have power; and the little child, as well as the grown man, may possess this power, and exercise it in winning souls for Jesus. A little girl who had bowed at the altar and given her heart to God, pulled the pastor's coat at the close of the service, and said, "Will you please pray for my mamma?" "Certainly," said the pastor. And the next evening the little girl brought her mother to the service. When the invitation was given, she took her hand and led her to the altar. That little girl's faith won her mother to Christ.

Faith will give courage for personal work. With a strong, unfaltering confidence which takes God at his word, we shall not hesitate nor fear to approach the unsaved and seek to win them to the Savior.

Faith is nourished by the Word. "Faith cometh by hearing, and hearing by the Word of God." If we feed our faith upon the Word, and exercise it, then we shall have the faith of those mentioned in the eleventh chapter of Hebrews, and we shall prove the promise of the Savior, "All things are possible to him that believeth."

STUDY XIV.

SELF-SACRIFICE.

Memory Verse: "For whosoever will save his life, shall lose it; and whosoever will lose his life for my sake, shall find it." — (Matt. xvi, 25.)

Scripture for Meditation: Matt. xvi, 24; 2 Cor. iv.

The words of Christ, "If any man will come after me, let him deny himself, and take up his cross, and follow me," can not be mistaken. The earthly life of Jesus was a supreme example of self-sacrifice. All the way from Bethlehem to Calvary his life was a constant denial of self. The early Church followed their Master. They were ready to sacrifice all. Men sold their fields and houses for the work's sake. They counted nothing too good for sacrifice, even to life itself; and many went gladly to the arena and the fiery stake rather than be untrue to their Lord. As long as the early Christian Church maintained this spirit, she went from victory to victory. Nothing could withstand her progress. And when the followers of Jesus Christ in this twentieth century shall again put on the beautiful garments of self-sacrifice, the Church will become invincible.

There is now a great opportunity for men and women to sacrifice, in personal liberty, in popularity, in social standing, and personal comfort, for the sake of the perishing multitudes. None are too poor, none too old, to do something to win souls.

An aged widow, who had all her money invested in a farm in a drouth-stricken part of the West, found herself almost penniless. She was compelled to find shelter in a Refuge Home. At first she was discouraged and heart-broken; but God put upon her heart the multitudes of perishing women in India. She tried to occupy her mind piecing a quilt. This she sold, and the money was sent to India. Then she made another for Africa, then another for Japan, until now, in six years, she has given four hundred dollars to home and foreign missions, and has six people at work as her substitutes in foreign lands. And she says, "I was surely called of God to teach that no one is too poor to give to missions, or too old to work for God and souls."

A young man, twenty-four years old, working on a farm for twenty dollars a month and board, has, in nineteen months, sent six substitutes, and says, "I pray God to make me a Christian drunkard, that I may spend my time and money for him as the drunkard does for the devil." And when the whole Church shall begin to show the same spirit of self-sacrifice in giving time and money, and in sacrificing pleasure and comfort and social standing for the Lord's work, and for dying multitudes about them, then we shall soon see the dawn of the millennial day.

THIRD WEEK -THE SOUL-WINNER'S EQUIPMENT.

"COMPLETELY FURNISHED."

STUDY XV.

KNOWLEDGE OF THE SCRIPTURES.

MEMORY VERSE: "Let the word of Christ dwell in you richly in all wisdom." — (Col. iii, 16.)

SCRIPTURE FOR MEDITATION: Heb. iv, 12; 2 Tim. iii, 13-17; Ps. cxix, 1-11.

A thorough knowledge of the Word of God is essential to success in soul-winning. The Word is "the sword of the Spirit," "the hammer that breaketh the rock in pieces." If we are not skilled in the use of the Divine sword and the Divine hammer, then we can not expect that the Spirit will use us.

In an excellent little book on "How to Obtain the Fullness of Power," Dr. R.A. Torrey says:

"There can be no fullness of life and service if the Bible is neglected. In much that is now written on power; also in much that is said in conventions, this fact is overlooked. The work of the Holy Spirit is magnified; but the instrument through which the Holy Spirit works is largely forgotten. The result is transient enthusiasm and activity, but no steady continuance and increase in power and usefulness. We can not obtain power, and we can not maintain power, in our own lives and in our work for others, unless there is deep and frequent meditation upon the Word of God.... Of course, it is much easier, and therefore much more agreeable to our spiritual laziness, to go to a convention or revival-meeting, and claim a 'filling with the Holy Spirit,' than it is to peg along, day after day, month after month, year after year, digging into the Word of God. But a 'filling of the Spirit,' that is not maintained by a persistent study of the Word will soon vanish.... Evidently Paul knew of no filling with the Spirit divorced from deep and constant meditation upon the Word."

The most remarkable movement among young men in this generation is the World's Christian Student Federation, organized by Mr. John R. Mott. Through this movement multitudes of young men the world over have been led to keep what is called "The Morning Watch," by which they rise at least half an hour earlier than usual each morning, and spend the time in devotional Bible-study and prayer. What a mighty impetus would be given to Christian work everywhere if all Christian young people would form the habit of keeping "The Morning Watch!"

Have a plan for your Bible study, and faithfully follow it. Commit to memory the texts found in Study Twenty-seven, and thus be able to use skillfully the Sword of the Spirit.

STUDY XVI.

TACT.

Memory Verse: "I am made all things to all men, that I might by all means save some." — (1 Cor. ix, 22.)

Scripture for Meditation: 1 Cor. ix, 19-27.

The successful business man knows the value of tact, and the Christian worker should know the value of consecrated tact. A special study of the life of Christ to notice his methods of dealing with various people, and to see the aptness with which he used parable and exhortation, would prove very helpful to every soul-winner. The life of Paul might also be studied in the same manner with profit. He knew how to become all things to all men to save some.

Christ's exhortation to his disciples was, "Be ye as wise as serpents," but how little wisdom many seem to have in seeking to win the unsaved to Christ! And this, too, when we have the promise, "If any of you lack wisdom, let him ask of God, that giveth to all men liberally, and upbraideth not: and it shall be given him."

"Now if I could tell you," said a pastor to an unsaved business man, who had been relating how much a friend had helped him in business, "how much Christ has helped me, and what he has been to me, I believe I could win you to him."

The value of tact was well illustrated in an incident which occurred during Mr. Finney's meetings in New York City. The big cutlery firm of Sheffield, England, had a branch house in New York. The manager was a partner of the firm, and very worldly. One of his clerks, who had been converted in the meetings, invited his employer to attend. One evening he was there, and sat just across the aisle from Mr. Arthur Tappan. He appeared affected during the sermon, and Mr. Tappan kept his eye on him. After the dismissal, Mr. Tappan stepped quickly across the aisle, introduced himself, and invited him to stay for the after-service. The gentleman tried to excuse himself and get away, but Mr. Tappan caught hold of the button on his coat and said, "Now, do stay; I know you will enjoy it;" and he was so kind and gentlemanly that the cutlery man could not very well refuse. He staid, and was converted. Afterwards he said, "An ounce of weight upon my coat-button saved my soul."

To watch for opportunity, and then to know how effectively to make use of the opportunity, is all-important in soul-winning. And there is no better teacher than the Holy Spirit, of whom it is said, "He shall teach you all things, and bring all things to your remembrance."

STUDY XVII.

EARNESTNESS.

Memory Verse: "Whatsoever thy hand findeth to do, do it with thy might." — (Eccl. ix, 10.)

Scripture for Meditation: Mark ii, 1-12.

The testimony of Charles H. Spurgeon should have weight here. He said: "If a man is to be a soul-winner, there must be in him intensity of emotion as well as sincerity of heart. You may repeat the most affectionate exhortations in such a half-hearted manner that no one will be moved either by love or fear. I believe that for soul-winning there is more in this matter of earnestness than in almost anything else."

When we become as much in earnest to rescue our friends and dear ones from eternal death as we are to save them from physical suffering and death, then we shall see the rapid spread of the kingdom of Christ. A man falls overboard from the deck of a vessel, and his wife screams: "Stop the boat! My God! My husband is drowning!" But no one criticises the woman for her passionate outcry, or bids her keep still. It was so natural for her to cry out for help. And when the Church of Jesus Christ becomes thoroughly awake to the worth of a soul and the awful danger to which all out of Christ are exposed, it will be the most natural thing in the world for them to show an undying earnestness in seeking the lost. Then propriety, and reticence, and restraint, and rules of rhetoric will be thrown to the winds, and a divine passion will possess the life. The world may sneer at it as fanaticism, but it is the fanaticism of Pentecost. When the crowd saw the intensity of emotion shown by the newly-anointed disciples, they exclaimed, "These men are full of new wine." Here was shown an enthusiasm that leaps over all difficulties and rises above every discouragement—the enthusiasm of Pentecost; and every soul-winner must have it. Then, like Paul, wishing himself accursed that Israel might be saved, or like John Welch, wrapped in his plaid, kneeling in the snow, unable to sleep, and praying mightily for the souls of men, this holy earnestness will not let us rest until we see the salvation of the lost.

It will tell in look, and tone, and manner. It may lead us to do things that may shock the sense of propriety of the dead, formal Church member, such as being obedient to the Master's command, "Go ye out into the highways and hedges, and compel them to come in." Jeremiah preached repentance in the streets; and the early Church preached everywhere, on the streets, by the river's bank, in the market-places, and in prisons. John Livingstone stood on a tombstone, and preached with such power in the midst of a falling rain that multitudes were born in a day. So did John Wesley. O that the great Church of Jesus Christ might now have the enthusiasm of Pentecost!

STUDY XVIII.

PERSEVERANCE.

MEMORY VERSE: "Ye that are the Lord's remembrancers, take no rest." —(Isa. lxii, 6, R.V.)

SCRIPTURE FOR MEDITATION: Luke xv, 1-10.

How we are willing to persevere to save our friends from physical suffering and death! No night is too long to watch, no sacrifice too great to make, no burden too heavy to bear, that the life of a loved one may be saved. But should we not be just as persistent in our efforts to save from eternal death those whom we love?

Perhaps we have no more illustrious example of devotion to soul-winning than evidenced in the life of Uncle John Vassar. Two incidents, related by the Rev. Walter B. Vassar, illustrate the perseverance with which he sought the perishing.

A young man was noticed to come night after night to revival-meetings, but would slip away before one could grasp his hand. Mr. Vassar felt he must see this soul, and walked five miles to the farm where he lived, arriving as the family was about to eat an early dinner, of which he was urged to partake. After being seated, the face of the young man not appearing in the family group, Mr. Vassar excused himself from the table, and hunted through all the farm-buildings where a man might possibly be in hiding. At last, when about to confess himself defeated, he walked to the further end of the corn-crib, and there, in an old hogshead, he found the fellow lying low. He confessed afterward that he had taken satisfaction in looking through the bunghole of the hogshead, in believing Uncle John would not find him there. But this "winner of souls," knowing his opportunity, leaped over by the side of the runaway, and then and there turned, as Charles Spurgeon has said, "the hogshead into a Bethel," and won a soul for heaven.

An Irish woman in a village was told about a strange man calling about her place, and affirmed he would not be kindly treated if he knocked at her door. Mr. Vassar, not knowing her feelings, came there in his visits, but the moment she saw he was the man—according to the description of him—she slammed the door in his face. He sat at once upon her doorstep and began to sing:

> "But drops of grief can ne'er repay
> The debt of love I owe."

In a few weeks she wanted admission into the Protestant Church, and all her experience was, "Those drops of grief, those drops of grief; I could not get over them."

See how men persevere to get rich or to gain political prestige! See how insurance agents, and book agents, and traveling men persevere in their efforts to convince men! They seek most favorable times, and then often go again and again. And shall we who win immortal souls be any less diligent?

STUDY XIX.

TENDERNESS.

Memory Verse: "I am the good Shepherd; the good Shepherd giveth his life for the sheep." — (John x, 12.)

Scripture for Meditation: Luke xv, 3-7; John x, 1-18.

What infinite depths of tenderness are revealed in these sweet parables of the Lost Sheep and the Good Shepherd! The tender, loving heart of the Savior goes out in eager compassion and pity for the straying. What boundless sympathy is revealed in the words, "He calleth his own sheep by name;" "He goeth after that which is lost;" "When he hath found it, he layeth it on his shoulders, rejoicing!" The seeker after souls must be like his Master. A heart ready to melt at the sight of human suffering and human need is necessary to successful soul-winning. There are many whose hearts are hardened by long years of rebellion against God; whose power of will is emasculated by long years of neglect; and they will never be saved until some earnest Christian worker shall find them, whose heart has been touched with the same sorrow that Jesus felt when he stood on the Mount of Olives weeping over Jerusalem.

J. Hudson Taylor, of the China Inland Mission, tells that when he was a college student he had charge of a man with a gangrenous foot. It was his duty to dress the man's foot every day. He soon learned that his patient was not a Christian, and had not been in a church for forty years. Such was his hatred of religion that he refused to go inside the church at his wife's funeral. Young Taylor made up his mind to speak to this man about his soul every time he visited him. The man cursed him, and refused to allow him to pray. The student persisted in presenting Christ until one day he said to himself, "It's no use," and was leaving the room. When he reached the door, he turned around and saw the man looking after him as if saying, "Why, you are going away to-day without speaking to me about Christ!" Then the young man burst into tears, and returning to the bedside, said: "Whether you wish me to or not, I must deliver my soul. Will you let me pray with you?" The man assented, began to weep, was converted. Mr. Taylor says, "God broke my heart, that through me he might break this wicked man's heart."

Ask now that the Holy Spirit may give you a tender heart, and make your eyes a fountain of tears, that, with the sympathy of Christ, you may seek the lost and perishing.

STUDY XX.

BURDEN FOR SOULS.

Memory Verse: "For I could wish that myself were accursed from Christ for my brethren." —(Rom. ix, 3.)

Scripture for Meditation: Gen. xviii, 16-33.

How the great heart of the Savior was burdened for the lost! See him standing on Olivet and weeping as he said: "O Jerusalem, Jerusalem, thou that killest the prophets, and stonest them which are sent unto thee, how often would I have gathered thy children together, even as a hen gathereth her chickens under her wings, and ye would not!"

Where there is no real soul-burden for sinners, there will be no revival. The early Church travailed in pain for the souls of dying men. One preacher said, "As I entered the pulpit, I could scarcely stand erect because of my concern for the people and solicitude for souls;" and another said, "I spent a whole night in prayer, and what I passed through was inexpressible." When we get a glimpse of the worth of a soul, and then of the death of a soul, and begin to realize that we stand between lost men and heaven or hell, then we shall have real concern, and the Lord will hear our prayer of intercession.

When Mr. Moody first went to London he preached in a Congregational Church, Sunday morning. There was no particular stir. That evening he spoke to a large audience of men in the same place, and scores expressed a desire to become Christians. He went to Dublin next day, but was recalled by a telegram saying that a great revival had broken out. And Mr. Moody accounts for this wonderful work of grace which followed by telling that, on that Sunday morning, a lady went home and told her invalid sister that Mr. Moody from America had preached. "I know what that means," said the invalid. "We are going to have a great revival. I have been praying for months that the Lord would send him here." She would not eat any dinner, but spent the day in fasting and prayer. The revival began in that invalid's room.

A gentleman waked his wife up at three o'clock in the morning to have her join him in prayer in behalf of a neighboring family who were unsaved; and at daybreak went to his neighbor's house to entreat them to yield to Christ.

When such concern for the perishing is manifested by the Church, there is sure to be a gracious ingathering.

STUDY XXI.

A PERSONAL PENTECOST.

Memory Verse: "But ye shall receive power, after that the Holy Ghost is come upon you: and ye shall be witnesses unto me both in Jerusalem, and in all Judea, and in Samaria, and unto the uttermost part of the earth." — (Acts i, 8.)

Scripture for Meditation: Acts ii, 1-4; xix, 1-6.

But, above all, the soul-winner must have *a personal Pentecost*. Christ does not send us alone to seek the lost. In the fifteenth and sixteenth chapters of St. John's Gospel, he definitely promises the Comforter. And again, on the day of his ascension, he bids his disciples tarry at Jerusalem until the Holy Ghost is come. Then as they waited, "with one accord in one place," "a sound from heaven as of a rushing mighty wind filled all the house where they were sitting, ... and they were all filled with the Holy Ghost." Since that day the one supreme qualification for Christ's witnesses is *the enduement with the Holy Ghost*. He will give a better knowledge of the Scriptures; he will re-enforce tact and earnestness and perseverance; he will give tenderness of heart and the burden for souls.

What a marvelous change the coming of the Spirit wrought in those waiting disciples! They had forsaken him; they had doubted his word; Peter had denied him. But now they all became flaming evangels, and "spake the word of God with boldness."

A personal Pentecost will help the soul-winner to overcome timidity, give utterance and a holy boldness, and make effective the words he speaks. It is the supreme need of the Church to-day. God wants men and women in every vocation of life who are Spirit-filled; and who, by diligent study of the Word of God, by prayer, and by Christian testimony, live a Spirit-filled life that is perennial.

The personal worker will succeed only when endued and empowered with the Holy Ghost. Dr. J. Wilbur Chapman tells of a young Irishman who was a member of his Church, and who had not had the educational advantages many young people have. Dr. Chapman says:

"With a heart burdened for the men of the city, I called together a few of the men of the Church, and laying before them the plan I had in mind, told them first of all that we could do nothing without the 'infilling of the Holy Ghost.'

"When this had been explained, I noticed this man leave the room. He did not return while the meeting was in session. When I sought him I found him in one of the lower rooms of the church, literally on his face before God. He was in prayer.

"I shall never forget his petition: 'O God, I plead with thee for this blessing!' then, as if God were showing him what was in the way, he said, 'My Father, I will give up every known sin, only I plead with thee for power;' and then, as if his individual sins were passing before him, he said again and again, 'I will give them up; I will give them up.' Then, without any emotion, he rose from his knees, turned his face heavenward, and simply said, 'And now I claim the blessing.'

"For the first time he became sensible of my presence, and with a shining countenance he reached out his hands to clasp mine. You could feel the very presence of the Spirit as he said, 'I have received him; I have received him!' And I believe he had, for in the next few months he led more than sixty men into the kingdom of God. His whole life had been transformed."

FOURTH WEEK -THE SOUL-WINNER'S METHODS.

"THAT I MAY, BY ALL MEANS, SAVE SOME."

STUDY XXII.

DIRECT APPROACH.

Memory Verse: "Jesus ... saith unto him, Go home to thy friends, and tell them how great things the Lord hath done for thee." — (Mark v, 19.)

Scripture for Meditation: John iv, 1-42.

John Vassar, than whom there has been no more successful soul-winner for a hundred years, accomplished his work through personal conversation, and declared that the best method of dealing with souls is to strike home at once with the most direct and searching question possible. Without a word of introduction he would say, "Have you experienced that great change called the new birth?" That question could not be easily evaded.

Study the methods of Christ in dealing with such as Nicodemus, the Samaritan woman, and the rich young man. How eagerly he used every opportunity! How his questions search the life! Without any apology, how he thrusts home warning and entreaty!

How easily we may lose opportunity to speak directly to men of their danger! While the great Dr. Chalmers was a guest at the home of his friend, a Highland country gentleman, his friend died suddenly. Dr. Chalmers had never spoken to him about his soul. He was much distressed, and said, "If I had only known that he was going to be taken from earth so soon, how earnestly I would have pleaded with him about his soul!"

Dr. J.E. Carson, of New York City, said to his congregation one Sunday morning, that every saved man was either a channel through which the Spirit of God was reaching the unsaved, or a barrier preventing the Spirit doing his work. One of the trustees of the Church said to himself on the way home, "Am I a channel, or a barrier?" That night he could not sleep, and cried out, "O Lord, make me a channel!" Almost the first thought that came was that there were some men in his employ to whom he had never spoken a word about Jesus Christ. He confessed his fault, and told the Lord that if he would make him a channel he would speak to these men. The first man who entered his office the next morning was his confidential clerk, who had been with him eighteen years. The merchant said, "Edward, haven't I been a good employer to you?" "Yes, sir." "Have not I treated you well?" "Yes, sir." "Why, sir, what have I done," said the clerk, "that you are going to discharge me?" "Edward, I am on my way to heaven, and I want you to go with me." Tears came into the eyes of both men as Edward took the merchant's extended hand and said, "I will, sir." Dr. Carson afterwards received eleven men into his Church because this trustee had consented to be a channel for the Holy Spirit.

Dr. Manley S. Hard talked with a physician about his soul, and, two days after, the doctor entered the revival-meeting just before the benediction, walked straight to the altar, and begged the people to wait and pray for him, saying:

"I know it is late and you are all tired, but I want you to stay a little while and pray for me. This has been an awfully hard day. I have ridden fifty miles and visited more than twenty patients, but I am the sickest man of them all. Two sermons have been preached to me; a faithful one yesterday by my pastor; the other this morning when I had to tell a woman she had better get ready to die, for she could not live. As I drove away I said to myself, 'You have warned another, but you are not ready yourself.'"

To go to a man and speak to him directly and plainly about his responsibility to God, and warn him to flee from "the wrath to come," may take more courage than to preach to a thousand; but it pays, and it must be done if the dying multitudes are ever saved.

STUDY XXIII.

CORRESPONDENCE.

MEMORY VERSE: "Ye see how large a letter I have written unto you with mine own hand." — (Gal. vi, 11.)

SCRIPTURE FOR MEDITATION: Philemon.

What a beautiful letter is that which Paul wrote to Philemon! How it breathes affection, and sympathy, and tender entreaty! And it was written *by his own hand*. Study this letter, and have your heart saturated with its spirit. You will then know how to write "words that touch" to your unsaved friends.

There are special occasions, such as the time of bereavement, of sickness, of trial, or of success, when this method may be employed to advantage. Many a soul has been won for Christ, and many a lonely life cheered by a sympathetic, wisely-worded letter, winged by prayer.

Sitting in a public park, a young man was seen poring over a letter while the tears rained down his face, and he almost sobbed aloud. "It is from my mother," he said. "She wrote it herself, and though I ran away from home and broke her heart, yet she says that she still loves me, and is praying for me, and wants me to come home."

Dr. T.L. Cuyler went to make his first call on a rich merchant. It was a cold winter evening, and as the door was opened when the minister was leaving, a cold, piercing gale swept in. Dr. Cuyler said, "What an awful night for the poor!" The merchant went back and brought a roll of bank-bills, saying, "Give these to the poorest people you know." Some days after, Dr. Cuyler wrote him, telling him how his bounty had relieved many poor, and then added, "How is it that a man so kind to his fellow-creatures has always been so unkind to his Savior as to refuse him his heart?" That sentence touched him. He sent for the minister to talk to him, was converted, and told Dr. Cuyler that he was the first person in twenty years who had spoken to him about his soul.

Do not allow letter-writing to excuse you from direct personal work; but watch for opportunity to write, as well as speak, that "by all means you may save some."

STUDY XXIV.

TRACTS AND BOOKS.

Memory Verse: "And when I looked, behold, a hand was sent unto
me; and, lo, a roll of a book was therein." — (Ezek. ii, 9.)

Scripture for Meditation: Eccl. xi, 1; 1 Tim. iv, 7-16.

The influence of a tract or of a good book can not be estimated. Rev. J. Hudson
Taylor, of the China Inland Mission, was converted in boyhood through reading a
gospel tract which he found in his father's library. "He had been frequently trou-
bled about his soul, and had again and again tried to become a Christian, but had
failed so often that he had concluded that there was no use in trying any more."

An agent of the American Tract Society relates the following:

"A man on a canal-boat received a tract, but to show his contempt for the tract
and its giver, took out his penknife and cut it up into fantastic shapes. Then he
held it up to the derision of the company.

"In tearing it apart, one of the pieces clung to his knee. His eyes were attract-
ed by the only word on it—'eternity.' He turned it over, and there was the word
'God.'

"These ideas remained in his mind. He tried to laugh them off; then to drink,
to play cards in order to banish them. But they still clung to him, and plagued him
till he sought God and preparation for eternity."

There is an old true story about a tract, that should be told over and over again:

A Puritan minister named Sibbs wrote a tract called "The Bruised Reed." A
copy of this was given by a humble layman to a little boy at whose father's house
he had been entertained over night. That boy was Richard Baxter, and the book
was the means of his conversion. Baxter wrote his "Call to the Unconverted," and
among the multitude led to Christ by it was Philip Doddridge. Doddridge wrote
"The Rise and Progress of Religion in the Soul," and "the time would fail to tell"
its blessed influence. By it Wilberforce was converted, and of his life and labors
volumes could be written. Wilberforce wrote his "Practical View of Christianity,"
and this led not only Dr. Chalmers into the truth, but Legh Richmond to Christ.
Richmond wrote "The Dairyman's Daughter," which has been published in a hundred languages, and many million copies have been sold.

But he who would make the best use of good literature must be wise. How
little tact some workers have! In a hospital a tract-distributor handed a leaflet on

dancing to a poor fellow who had lost both limbs. Another zealous young man gave a tract on "The Tobacco Habit" to a beautiful cultured lady, the wife of a minister. A good supply of common sense is just as necessary to success in the use of this method as in any other.

STUDY XXV.

THE PRAYER LIST.

Memory Verse: "I will pray for you unto the Lord." —(1 Sam. vii, 5.)

Scripture for Meditation: Luke xviii, 1-8.

One of the highest privileges of the Christian life is the privilege of intercession for the unsaved. Every Christian may be an intercessor, and bear to the mercy-seat, in the arms of prayer, some unsaved friend every day. Have a prayer list. In a little memorandum-book write the names of those whom you are anxious to see saved. Spread these names before the Lord daily until your prayers are answered.

One of the greatest Christian movements of modern times started with a prayer-list carried in the vest-pocket of a commercial traveler, Mr. E.R. Graves, traveling for a paper-house in New York City. He secured permission from a merchant to allow his name to be entered on his prayer-list. The merchant wrote his name in the traveler's book, and then proceeded to inform Mr. Graves that he had determined not to be a Christian, and that he had taken too big a contract if he expected to pray him into the kingdom. But the traveler simply said, "I confidently expect my prayer to be answered." When they met again the merchant had been converted, and, amid tears of rejoicing, another name was checked off the list. The merchant's name was Samuel M. Sayford. Mr. Sayford became a secretary in the Young Men's Christian Association, and shortly after met C.K. Ober, then a student at Williams College, and pushed him out into Association work. Mr. Ober, in turn, found John E. Mott in Cornell University, persuaded him to enter Association work among students; and Mr. Mott, in the course of time, started on his journey around the world, organizing the World's Christian Student Federation.

STUDY XXVI.

WORK AMONG STUDENTS.

Memory Verse: "Now then we are ambassadors for Christ, as though God did beseech you by us: we pray you in Christ's stead, be ye reconciled to God." —(2 Cor. v, 20.)

Scripture for Meditation: 1 Cor. ii.

No more fruitful and important field for personal work can be found than in our educational institutions, and Christian students who make soul-winning a habit of life may win many rich trophies for the Master. Bishop H.W. Warren, when a Freshman in college, was led to an open confession of Christ through a Saturday morning walk with a Junior, who talked to him about his soul.

Dr. J.W. Bashford, in *The Christian Student*, tells about "a Senior in the Ohio Wesleyan University who was smitten with conviction because he had neglected personal work for the Master. He intended to be a minister, but had been indifferent to the spiritual welfare of his student friends. He offered himself to Christ in full consecration, and made a list of sixteen friends for whom he felt personal responsibility. He engaged in systematic personal work with these friends, and had the satisfaction before the year was completed of seeing every one of them begin the Christian life. Six of his sixteen friends entered the ministry, and some of them are even more talented and successful than the student friend who led them to Christ."

As a rule, young people during their college years are thoughtful and easily reached; but if not saved before they leave the college halls and begin the active work of life, they are almost certainly lost to the kingdom. How often, because of timidity or carelessness, Christian students and teachers allow this precious harvest time to go by, and lose the opportunity to win a soul for Christ!

A man, who is now an eminent and widely-known minister, says that he roomed with a young man at college for two years, and never said a word to him about his soul. When he was about to leave for home, his room-mate said, "Why have you not spoken to me about my soul?" Said the Christian student, "I thought you did not care for me to do so." The young man replied, "Why, that is the very reason I roomed with you, and there has never been a day for these two years that you could not have done so."

Let Christian students set out to win some trophies among their friends and room-mates for Christ. The results of faithful personal work may not be immediate or apparent, but the blessed Spirit of God will water the seed. For thirteen months a college student prayed for and urged a fellow-student to surrender to Christ, and died without seeing any result of his efforts. But the seed was faithfully sown, and the young man was afterwards converted, and became Bishop Hannington, the martyr bishop of Africa.

STUDY XXVII.

MEETING OBJECTIONS.

Memory Verse: "For I will give you a mouth and wisdom, which all your adversaries shall not be able to gainsay nor resist." —(Luke xxi, 15.)

Scripture for Meditation: John ix, 1-41.

The zealous personal worker will be met by objections; but it must be remembered that these objections are often given for the sake of argument, and often for the sake of something to say. They should be squarely met, however, and answered; and the best way to answer such is by Scripture. There is not an objection advanced by the unconverted that can not be met and overcome by some passage of Scripture. Just as Jesus in the wilderness met the tempter's arguments with "It is written," so we may meet every argument of the objector with the Word.

A faithful study of Christ's conversations with seeking souls, such as Nicodemus and the rich young man, will also be helpful.

Below are some of the objections usually given, with the Scripture references that may be used to meet them. This arrangement of texts is taken from "Personal Work," by S.M. Sayford, by consent of the publishers:

"I am good enough." (Gen. vi, 5; Ps. li, 5-7; Luke xviii, 19.)

"I am as good as most Christians." (Rom. xiv, 10-12; 2 Cor. v, 10; Rev. xx, 11; xii, 15.)

"I have never done anything really bad." (Luke xvi, 15; James ii, 10.)

"I can not give up my pleasures." (Eccl. ii, 1; xi, 9; Ps. xvi, 11.)

"I know I shall fail." (John vi, 37; 2 Tim. i, 12; iv, 18.)

"I can not now, but will some time." (Luke xiv, 17; Acts xxiv, 25; James iv, 13, 14; Luke xii, 19, 20.)

"I am too great a sinner." (Luke v, 32; xix, 10; 1 Tim. i, 15.)

"My day of grace has past." (Ex. xxxiv, 5-7; 2 Chron. xxx, 9; Isa. lv, 7.)

"I do not feel concerned." (Rom. xiii, 11; Eph. v, 14; Heb. ii, 3.)

"I can not know that these things are true." (Acts xvii, 11; John v, 39; vii, 17.)

"It will cost me my living." (Matt. vi, 33; Ps. lxxxiv, 11; Rom. xiv, 8.)

"It will prevent my becoming rich." (1 Tim. vi, 9, 10; Mark viii, 36, 37; Rev. iii, 17, 18.)

"I can not hold my friends." (Matt. x, 37; xxii, 37; Phil. iii, 8.)

"How may I know that Christ is the Son of God?" (John xx, 30, 31; x, 23-25; 1 John v, 13, 20; Mark iv, 11.)

"How may I know that the Bible is true?" (John vii, 17.)

"Will not God save me if I do my best?" (Eph. ii, 9; Titus iii, 5-8.)

"Why must a man believe in Christ to be saved?" (John xiv, 6; Acts iv, 12; Gal. ii, 16; Rom. iii, 23, 26.)

"How may I know I am forgiven?" (Ps. xxxii, 5; Prov. xxviii, 13; 1 John i, 7-9.)

STUDY XXVIII.

NO EFFORT IN VAIN.

Memory Verse: "So shall my word be that goeth forth out of my mouth: it shall not return unto me void, but it shall accomplish that which I please, and it shall prosper in the thing whereto I sent it." —(Isa. lv, 11.)

Scripture for Meditation: John iv, 36; 1 Cor. xv, 58.

"Some day I hope you will preach the gospel," said an aged minister to a little boy in England. That boy became Charles H. Spurgeon. That great soul-winner, Mark Guy Pearse, says that when he was a boy his father took him to see a saintly old lady, who laid her hand upon his head, saying, "God bless the boy, and make him a minister." Mr. Pearse says that, through this aged woman, God called him to the ministry.

In a college chapel in Pennsylvania a Christian layman sat down beside a boy and talked to him about Christ. That boy became Alfred Cookman, whose name will be held in everlasting remembrance.

An eminent lawyer of Minneapolis, converted a short time since, declares that the earnest question, "Have you found Jesus?" spoken by a young lady to his friend who sat by his side in a revival-meeting, and her startled look, when she was answered roughly, followed him for fifteen years until he was finally converted.

No sincere effort for Christ can fail. To human eyes there may be little encouragement, but his Word shall prevail. Every invitation and entreaty shall in the end be, to those who reject it, the "savor of death unto death," but to those who accept it, "the savor of life unto life." We may go forth now, weeping, bearing precious seed; but some blessed day we shall doubtless come again with rejoicing, bringing our sheaves with us.

Perhaps we are too anxious to see results now. We do like to number the converts, and add to the Church roll. Far better do our best for Christ and souls, then leave the results to God. He will see that the seed, faithfully planted, is watered, and that no effort is in vain.

Lector House believes that a society develops through a two-fold approach of continuous learning and adaptation, which is derived from the study of classic literary works spread across the historic timeline of literature records. Therefore, we aim at reviving, repairing and redeveloping all those inaccessible or damaged but historically as well as culturally important literature across subjects so that the future generations may have an opportunity to study and learn from past works to embark upon a journey of creating a better future.

This book is a result of an effort made by Lector House towards making a contribution to the preservation and repair of original ancient works which might hold historical significance to the approach of continuous learning across subjects.

HAPPY READING & LEARNING!

LECTOR HOUSE LLP
E-MAIL: lectorpublishing@gmail.com

www.ingramcontent.com/pod-product-compliance
Lightning Source LLC
Chambersburg PA
CBHW051501140726
47987CB00006B/2833